Who's Hiding in This Book?

Meet Ten Famous Authors

by Sheila Cordner
Illustrated by Daniel Fiore

For Thomas and Connor, with love.
—S.C.

For Sara, who never stops believing in me.
—D.F.

———————————————————————————

Who's Hiding in This Book?

Copyright © 2019

Author: Sheila Cordner

Illustrator: Daniel Fiore

Publisher: Pierce Press / Gigglequick Books

PiercePress.com

Member: Independent Publishers of New England

Member: Independent Book Publishers Association

Softcover ISBN: 978-0-9960975-6-7

Hardcover ISBN: 978-0-9960975-8-1

Library of Congress Catalog Number pending

Book Layout & Design: Encircle Publications

Editing: Allison Wortche

Copy Editing and Proofreading: Shasta Clinch and Anna Juraschek

Cover Illustration: Daniel Fiore, *DanielFiore.com*

Layout & Design: Eddie Vincent, Encircle Publications

Page count: 34 pages

Trim size: 11 x 8.5 inches

Printed by Lightning Source (Ingram)

Distributed by Ingram and Pierce Press

Please contact the publisher for reprint rights, foreign rights, and other business matters at info@piercepress.com.

Can you see them?

Look carefully, and you'll discover that hiding in every book you read is an author.

Authors can be funny, daring, or shy. Some tell stories based on their own lives. Others use their imagination.

All the authors you'll meet here wrote important books.

Are you ready? Let's go meet them!

Who will we find in the bright lights of New York City?

I am Langston Hughes.

As a young man, I wanted to be an engineer. But when I moved to Harlem in New York City, I met writers, musicians, and artists. I discovered writing was what I loved most.

BLUES

JAZZ DANCING

Live Music

In my poem "The Weary Blues,"
I write about playing the piano.
"Rocking back and forth," a pianist
plays songs so beautiful that
anyone hearing them rises up and
dances. Together, old neighbors
and new friends wiggle their
bodies to the sounds of the blues.
They hear the piano long
into the night.

Next, let's dive into the sea. . .

I am Herman Melville.

I spent my days at sea—on a merchant
ship and a whaling boat—
before I became an author.

In my novel *Moby Dick*, I write about
searching for a white whale.

We won't stop until we find him. *SPLASH!* Finally, he jumps out of the water. "His spout is a big one!" the captain shouts. He's larger than our boat! But the whale cannot be caught. He disappears back into the waves.

Now bundle up! It's time to make snow angels . . .

I am Zitkála-Šá (Red Bird).

Most people know me as a writer, but I was also a musician. I studied violin at the New England Conservatory of Music, and even performed in Paris!

In my story "The School Days of an Indian Girl," I write about leaving my reservation for a new school.

At first, I'm nervous—so many new faces, so many people I don't know.
But then . . . it begins to snow.

Even though we get in a little bit of trouble, my classmates and I have "great sport in the snow," throwing snowballs and making snow angels! I miss my home, but my classmates start to feel like friends.

Listen! Do you hear a woodpecker?

I am Emily Dickinson.

I lived at my family's homestead in Massachusetts while writing my almost 1,800 poems.

In my poems, I write about nature—berries and blossoms, birds and bumblebees.

I admire the determined woodpecker,
searching and pecking,
"a Worm, His utmost Goal."
He drills his beak into
every inch of the tree's bark.
There it is!
He finds the worm.

Ready to board an airplane to Egypt? Prepare for takeoff!

I am Taha Hussein.

I grew up in a small village in Egypt.

When I was thirteen years old, I went to school in Cairo to study the Quran. But I *really* wanted to learn about famous works of literature, so I went on to the University of Cairo and the Sorbonne in Paris.

Eventually, I told my own stories that people around the world wanted to read! In "An Egyptian Childhood," part of my memoir, I write about being blind and how this challenge helped me use my imagination. I was eager to explore my neighborhood. I imagined becoming a rabbit! If I were a rabbit, I could "traverse the fence by leaping over it." I was desperate to discover freedom in the larger world.

Together, let's search the streets of London . . .

I am Virginia Woolf.

I am known for my feminist ideas, and I believe that women writers need quiet spaces of our own in order to create masterpieces.

In my book *Flush*, I imagine what it is like to be a dog. Flush, a cocker spaniel, runs through the loud streets of London. He dodges horses and leaps over market carts.

He sprints like a cheetah, the fastest land animal in the world! Flush enjoys his independence but soon starts to miss his family.

He sniffs until he detects a familiar scent. It's the mahogany door to his house at 50 Wimpole Street! He rushes inside and "springs on to the sofa." His owner hugs him until he falls asleep in the warm living room.

Now, let's climb into a covered wagon to cross the United States . . .

I am María Amparo Ruiz de Burton.

I grew up in California in the 1800s, speaking both Spanish and English. I later became one of the first published Mexican-American authors.

In my novel *Who Would Have Thought It*, I write about a brave twelve-year-old girl named Lola, who travels across the United States in a covered wagon to her unknown life in New England. Lola looks different from the people on the East Coast, and they are slow to

accept her as a friend—until they learn what she's brought with her. Her new neighbors have never seen so many sparkling jewels! They ask, "Is it *real* gold?" She tells them the story of how her mother discovered the treasure while swimming in the Colorado River. They are interested in her jewels, but Lola is more interested in their friendship.

Join us! Our horse-drawn carriage rattles through Central Park . . .

I am Edith Wharton.

As a child, I lived in grand houses in New York City, Newport, and Europe. When I grew up, I designed a lavish home and called it "The Mount." Built in the Berkshire Mountains of Massachusetts, it has been preserved as a museum so others can see it!

In my novel *The Age of Innocence*, I write about Central Park in 1800s New York City. Some people speed through on bicycles. Some visit on foot. But the *best* way to see the park is slowly, "in one's own carriage." Impeccably groomed horses know every winding road. *Neigh! Neigh!* they say to each other as they lead us down tree-lined paths.

Pull on your hiking boots! Who will we find in the woods?

My name is Henry David Thoreau.

I escaped the busy life in town to enjoy the simple life in the forest. I lived in a one-room cabin, and I only returned to my mother's house when I needed clean clothes! In my book *Walden*, I write about living "alone, in the woods."

I have no human neighbors, but I never *feel* alone because I am surrounded by animals. I invite my fox friends for dinner. Together we dine on berries! When my mice buddies come to visit, I offer them tiny pieces of my bread. Far away from the city, I learn about the mysterious habits of these small creatures.

Take a deep breath before we climb the hilly streets of San Francisco . . .

I am Sui Sin Far.

My father was British, and my mother was Chinese. I was born in England and moved to the United States when I was six. I wrote about the lives of Chinese immigrants.

龍舟

移民

In my story "Mrs. Spring Fragrance," a woman learns to mix ancient Chinese ways with new traditions. She helps her "honorable cousin prepare for the Fifth Moon Festival" in San Francisco. They watch Dragon Boat races and eat dumplings! She makes American fudge so they can feast on both traditional Chinese food and American treats.

Together, we've traveled far! We've danced in New York City, sailed on a whaling ship, visited an Egyptian village, wandered the streets of London, and more!

Now that we've finished our journey to meet ten writers, where will we find the next great author? Who might it be?

Will it be YOU?

BECOME AN AUTHOR!

What story do you want to tell?

I am _____

If I wrote a book, it would be about _____
_____
_____
_____
_____

It's important to me because _____
_____
_____
_____

On the cover of my book, there would be a picture of _____
_____
_____
_____

Five people I would want to read my book are _____
_____
_____
_____
_____

I think they would like it because _____
_____
_____
_____
_____

GUIDE FOR PARENTS AND EDUCATORS

Visit sheilacordner.com for new and updated resources and children's activities!

LANGSTON HUGHES (1902-1967)

"The Weary Blues" (1926)

Food for Thought: Langston Hughes was an influential part of the Harlem Renaissance movement in the early twentieth century. His essay, "The Negro Artist and the Racial Mountain," argues that black writers and musicians should create their own forms of expression, like jazz and blues music.

Discuss with Children: Introduce the idea of poetry and connect it to the rhythms of music. Read Hughes's poem "The Weary Blues," for example, in which you can hear the musical quality of his words in each line's rhymes and rhythm.

Words to Learn: Engineer, The Blues, Pianist

HERMAN MELVILLE (1819-1891)

***Moby Dick* (1851)**

Food for Thought: In addition to working on boats, Melville also worked on his uncle's farm; in a bank; as a teacher in a school; and in his family's felt and fur business. In the nineteenth-century, when Melville wrote *Moby Dick*, whaling was a profitable business; whale oil was used for oil lamps, for example. Now, most countries ban the capturing of whales.

Discuss with Children: Use the story of how Captain Ahab relentlessly pursues Moby Dick—the enormous sperm whale who eludes him—as a way to talk about how humans cannot always control the awe-inspiring forces of nature.

Words to Learn: Whaling Boat, Merchant Ship

ZITKÁLA-ŠÁ (RED BIRD) (1876-1938)

"The Schooldays of an Indian Girl" (1900)

Food for Thought: Zitkála-Šá, who also went by the names Red Bird and Gertrude Bonnin, was from South Dakota; her mother was a Sioux and her father was white. She attended a Quaker school in Indiana and later studied music at the New England Conservatory of Music.

Discuss with Children: Talk about what it might feel like to go to a new school. You could also attend a Native American cultural event together.

Words to Learn: Reservation, "Indian" vs. "Native American"

EMILY DICKINSON (1830-1886)

"His Bill an Augur is" (1865)

Food for Thought: Emily Dickinson's poems, which depict the everyday life of 1800s America, remind us to stop and appreciate the simple beauties in nature. Her poems have an almost meditative quality and encourage us to respect animals. Here is the poem, sometimes referred to as "The Woodpecker," in its entirety:

"His Bill an Augur is
His Head, a Cap and Frill
He laboreth at every Tree
A Worm, His utmost Goal - "

Discuss with Children: Ask children what other examples they see of animals determined to reach their goal, and for examples from their own lives of reaching a goal, big or small.

Words to Learn: Homestead, Determined, Woodpecker, Drill, Utmost

TAHA HUSSEIN (1889-1973)

An Egyptian Childhood (1929)

Food for Thought: Hussein grew up in northern Egypt and became blind when he was two years old. He initially embarked on studying the Quran but later became a scholar and writer of non-religious works. He received a Ph.D. from the newly formed Egyptian University—now Cairo University—and returned as a professor and dean. Hussein was nominated multiple times for the Nobel Prize in Literature; he wrote novels, stories, and essays, but his autobiography became his most well-known work outside of Egypt. *An Egyptian Childhood* was originally published in 1929 as the first section of *Al Ayyām*—translated to *The Days*—but then republished on its own in an English translation in 1932. Hussein discusses his experience with blindness, his feeling of being different from the rest of his family, and his education.

Discuss with Children: In addition to discussing Egypt, you could also talk about Hussein's determination to work hard and not let his blindness hold him back.

Words to Learn: Egypt, Quran, Cairo, Desperate, Traverse, Disability

VIRGINIA WOOLF (1882-1941)

Flush (1933)

Food for Thought: In *A Room of One's Own*, Woolf explores the advantages men have had over women. She stresses the importance of a woman writer having financial means and access to a room of her own. Many of her novels are serious and more abstract like *To the Lighthouse* or *Mrs. Dalloway*; *Flush* is her most playful book. Virginia Woolf learned about the real-life dog, Flush, by reading the famous love letters between Victorian poet Elizabeth Barrett Browning and her husband, poet Robert Browning. Robert Browning wrote to Elizabeth Barrett at her house at 50 Wimpole Street in London before they eloped against her father's wishes. Woolf was fascinated by their love story and decided to write a biography focused on Elizabeth Barrett Browning's dog.

Discuss with Children: Encourage children to think about how animals can become such important members of families. Ask: What things would you include in a "biography"—or story—about your own pet or another animal?

Words to Learn: Feminist, Empower, Masterpiece, Dodge, Detect

MARÍA AMPARO RUIZ DE BURTON (1832-1895)

Who Would Have Thought It? (1872)

Food for Thought: María Amparo Ruiz de Burton is considered the first Mexican-American author to write novels in English. Her Civil War-era novel, *Who Would Have Thought It*, chronicles the life of a young girl, Lola, whose Mexican mother has been captured by a Native American tribe. The mother asks a New England doctor who visits the tribe to bring her daughter to live with his family in New England. Lola's mother gives him diamonds and gold that she has acquired and instructs that he use it to pay for Lola's education until he can locate her father. When the doctor arrives with Lola in New England, his abolitionist and supposedly open-minded family and friends disrespect her because they think she is black or Native American. When they find out that Lola is an heiress to a fortune, consisting of the diamonds and gold her mother discovered in the Colorado River, they begin to try to win her favor. Ruiz de Burton exposes the racism and hypocrisy of Northeast society, which she experienced firsthand as an outsider. She grew up in Baja, California, where her grandfather had led the Mexican army. During the Mexican-American war, she met a commander of American troops, whom she later married, and they moved to the east coast.

Discuss with Children: Discuss the ways Mexican and American culture and history are related. What does it feel like to be an outsider?

Words to Learn: Mexican-American, Sparkling, Colorado River, Friendship

EDITH WHARTON (1862-1937)

The Age of Innocence (1920)

Food for Thought: In 1921, Wharton became the first woman to receive the Pulitzer Prize for Fiction, awarded for *The Age of Innocence*. She was known for drawing upon her own experiences as a member of the privileged class to comment on the bourgeoisie and upper classes of nineteenth-century American society.

Discuss with Children: Young readers could have fun imagining what life in American cities—such as New York City—was like in the 1800s and early 1900s, with horse-drawn carriages and muddy streets. How do cities look different today?

Words to Learn: Lavish, Preserved, Horse-drawn Carriage

HENRY DAVID THOREAU (1817-1862)

Walden (1854)

Food for Thought: Thoreau is known for his experiment living in a one-room cabin for two years in the woods. He built his cabin on property owned by his friend Ralph Waldo Emerson. He writes about this in *Walden*:

"When I wrote the following pages, or rather the bulk of them, I lived alone, in the woods, a mile from any neighbor, in a house which I had built myself, on the shore of Walden Pond, in Concord, Massachusetts, and earned my living by the labor of my hands only. I lived there two years and two months."

Today many people look to Thoreau and visit Walden Pond to foster a connection with nature in the midst of a hectic world. Some people use the writings of Thoreau as a reminder of the need for conservation. The site of his cabin has been preserved in Walden Pond State Reservation in Massachusetts, where you can visit and go swimming in the same pond in which he swam.

Discuss with Children: Ask children what they enjoy about being outside as a way of initiating a conversation about what it means to respect nature. Why is conservation important?

Words to Learn: Escape, Mysterious, Walden Pond

SUI SIN FAR (1865-1914)

Mrs. Spring Fragrance (1912)

Food for Thought: Her readers know her as Sui Sin Far (which means water lily or narcissus in Cantonese), but her given name was Edith Maude Eaton. After emigrating to New York with her family from England, she lived in Montreal and Jamaica before moving to California and later Boston. Sui Sin Far was known for her writing about the experiences of Chinese immigrants in the United States, which often called into question common stereotypes of Chinese immigrants and Chinese Americans.

Discuss with Children: Many families have traditions. What are some of yours? Discuss what it means to be an immigrant, and how immigration is a part of American history.

Words to Learn: Immigrants, Tradition, Fifth Moon Festival (Dragon Boat Festival)

BIBLIOGRAPHY

Here are some resources I found helpful in writing this book. Please see sheilacordner.com for live links to the following websites and additional resources suitable for children in this age range.

Academy of American Poets. "Emily Dickinson." Accessed April 19, 2019.
  poets.org/poetsorg/poet/emily-dickinson

Hughes, Langston. "The Negro Artist and the Racial Mountain." *The Nation*, June 23, 1926.
  thenation.com/article/negro-artist-and-racial-mountain/

Hussein, Taha. *The Days: His Autobiography in Three Parts*. Translated by E. H. Paxton, Hilary Wayment, and Kenneth Cragg. Cairo: The American University in Cairo Press, 2014.

"Langston Hughes." The Poetry Foundation. Accessed April 19, 2019.
  poetryfoundation.org/poets/langston-hughes

Lee, Hermione. *Edith Wharton*. New York: Knopf, 2007.

Lee, Hermione. *Virginia Woolf*. New York: Vintage, 1997.

Lewandowski, Tadeusz. *Red Bird, Red Power: The Life and Legacy of Zitkála-Šá*. Norman: University of Oklahoma Press, 2016.

Library of America. "Edith Maude Eaton, 'Mrs. Spring Fragrance.'" Last modified March 2, 2018.
  loa.org/news-and-views/1385-edith-maude-eaton-mrs-spring-fragrance

Montes, Amelia María, and Anne Elizabeth Goldman, Eds. *María Amparo Ruiz de Burton: Critical and Pedagogical Perspectives*. Lincoln: University of Nebraska Press, 2004.

The Mount: Edith Wharton's Home. "Edith Wharton: A Biography." Accessed April 19, 2019.
  edithwharton.org/discover/edith-wharton

Parker, Hershel. *Herman Melville: A Biography*, 2 vols. Baltimore: Johns Hopkins University Press, 2002.

PBS American Experience. "The Life of Herman Melville." Accessed April 19, 2019.
  pbs.org/wgbh/americanexperience/features/whaling-biography-herman-melville

Rampersad, Arnold. *The Life of Langston Hughes, Vol. I: 1902-1941, I, Too, Sing America*. New York: Oxford University Press, 2002.

Sewall, Richard B. *The Life of Emily Dickinson*. Cambridge: Harvard University Press, 1998.

"Ṭāhā Ḥusayn." Encyclopaedia Brittanica. Accessed April 19, 2019.
  britannica.com/biography/Taha-Husayn

The Walden Woods Project. "Henry David Thoreau." Accessed April 19, 2019.
  walden.org/thoreau

Walls, Laura Dassow. *Henry David Thoreau: A Life*. Chicago: University of Chicago Press, 2017.

White-Parks, Annette. *Sui Sin Far/Edith Maude Eaton: A Literary Biography*. Champaign: University of Illinois Press, 1995.

Woolf, Virginia. *A Room of One's Own*. New York: Mariner, 2005.

QUOTATION SOURCES

There are quotations from each author hidden throughout this book. Can you find them in the story?

rocking back and forth
Hughes, Langston. *The Collected Poems of Langston Hughes*. Edited by Arnold Rampersad. New York: Vintage Classics, 1995, p. 50.

his spout is a big one!
Melville, Herman. *Moby-Dick*. Third Edition. Edited by Hershel Parker. New York: Norton, 2017, p. 132.

great sport in the snow
Zitkála-Šá. "The School Days of an Indian Girl." *American Indian Stories, Legends, and Other Writings by Zitkála-Šá*. New York: Penguin Classics, 2003, p. 92.

a worm his utmost goal
Dickinson, Emily. "His Bill an Augur is. J 1034/F 990." *The Poems of Emily Dickinson: Reading Edition*. Edited by R.W. Franklin. Cambridge: The Belknap Press of Harvard University Press, 2005, p. 413.

traverse the fence by leaping over it
Hussein, Taha. *The Days: His Autobiography in Three Parts*. Translated by E.H. Paxton, Hilary Wayment, and Kenneth Cragg. Cairo: The American University in Cairo Press, 2014, p. 7.

springs...on to the sofa
Woolf, Virginia. *Flush*. New York: Harvest Books, 1983, p. 23.

is it real gold?
Ruiz De Burton, María Amparo. *Who Would Have Thought It?* New York: Penguin, 2009, p. 17.

in one's own carriage
Wharton, Edith. *The Age of Innocence*. Edited by Candace Waid. New York: Norton, 2003, p. 3.

alone, in the woods
Thoreau, Henry David. *Walden, Civil Disobedience, and Other Writings*. Third Edition. Edited by William Rossi. New York: Norton, 2008, p. 5.

honorable cousin prepare...for the Fifth Moon Festival
Far, Sui Sin. *Mrs. Spring Fragrance and Other Writings (1912)*. Edited by Amy Ling and Annette White-Parks. Champaign: University of Illinois Press, 1995, p. 21.

Meet the Author and Illustrator

Sheila Cordner, Ph.D., *author*

Sheila teaches literature at Boston University and lives in the Boston area with her husband and two young children. Her passion is to share her love of the classics with a broad audience. Her previous publications include a book on nineteenth-century authors' innovative ideas about education, and she has presented her research at national and international conferences. She believes we are never too young—or too old!—to appreciate great works of literature and bring diverse new ones to light.

Daniel Fiore, *illustrator*

After an art-filled childhood, Daniel attended Rochester Institute of Technology (RIT), where he discovered his passion for illustration. Daniel uses gouache and watercolor as well as mixed media consisting of colored pencil, oil, acrylic, "whatever medium best communicates the story." He especially enjoys creating portraits and caricatures. Recently, his focus has shifted towards children's book illustration, and he is thrilled to have contributed to this book, which helps communicate such an important message to today's youth.